Smugglers' Cove

Smugglers' Cove

by
BILL MANNING

Beacon Hill Press of Kansas City
Kansas City, Missouri

Copyright 2002
by Beacon Hill Press of Kansas City

Printed in the United States of America

ISBN 083-411-9390

Cover Design: Keith Alexander
Illustrator: Dick Wahl

Editor: Donna Manning
Associate Editor: Kathleen M. Johnson

Note: This is a fictional account of actual events. It is part of the *Understanding Christian Mission,* Children's Mission Education curriculum. It is designed for use in Year 2, The Bible and Mission. Lessons focus on the Bible and how it helps missionaries tell others about God's love.

10 9 8 7 6 5 4 3 2 1

Contents

1

I Hate Lizards!

"Run, Kim! Run! Don't let them catch you!" Lee was running and yelling at the top of his voice.

"Stop! Stop!" The two police officers were gaining on Kim and Lee.

The two boys crossed a footbridge. The path turned to the right, but the boys made a sharp turn to the left. Kim and Lee ran into the thicket of trees. Then they turned again and ran into the high bushes that lined the edge of the stream.

When the boys heard the sound of the officers' feet hitting the wooden planks of the old bridge, they crouched in the mud, under the cover of the bushes. The policemen came to the end of the bridge and followed the boys' path into the thicket. But the officers ran right on past the bushes.

Lee and Kim were crawling back to the path when a lizard crawled off of a bush onto Kim's head. Lee's eyes widened as he pointed at Kim's passenger. But pointing was unnecessary. Kim could already see the lizard's tail dangling between his eyes. Kim froze on his hands and knees. He closed his eyes tightly and whispered, "I hate lizards!"

As Lee sprang to his feet, he brushed the lizard off of Kim's head and into the bushes. Then Lee darted back over the bridge. But as Kim jumped up, he tripped and fell to the ground with a thud. The officers turned at the sound and saw Kim stumbling across the bridge. The chase was on again.

Just as Lee and Kim came to the road, the officers yelled out, "Bang! Bang!" Kim slumped to the ground, but Lee turned the corner and kept running.

"Lee," the officer yelled. "Lee, I got you! You're not playing fair!"

As Lee strolled back around the corner, he taunted his 10-year-old brother, "Bin, you didn't shoot me! You didn't even come close! Isn't that right, Yung?"

Yung, who had been playing the part of the other policeman, threw up his hands. "Don't ask me! I had my eyes closed!"

Lee protested, "Bin couldn't hit an elephant."

Then Kim gave a funny look and wrinkled his nose. "Well, how is it that he got me?"

"That was just luck. He was actually aiming at the lizard on your head!" Lee replied. Kim and Yung laughed out loud, but Bin failed to see the humor.

Before Bin had a chance to reply, Mrs. Chang stepped outside and called the boys. "Lee. Bin. It's time to eat."

Each of the boys knew what the call meant. Time for playing had officially ended. The boys headed toward their homes.

Just as Bin ran past Lee, three trucks rumbled along the road, stirring up clouds of dust. Bin kept on running, determined to get home before his 12-year-old brother. But Lee turned toward his two friends, Kim and Yung, with a puzzled look. "Something must be going on at the cove," he said.

"Yeah," Kim said. "Something's up."

Yung nodded in agreement, as they all stood looking down the road toward the beach. They could see the trucks moving closer to the cove.

"See if your folks will let you camp out with me tonight at the cave. That will give us a chance to check things out," Lee said.

"All right!" exclaimed Kim and Yung.

The three boys always had fun camping at the cave. Of course, it wasn't really a cave. That is what they called it. It was an area right behind their homes protected by an overhanging rock ledge. The cave was a great place for playing, camping, and talking with friends.

As Kim and Yung raced each other up the hill, they called out to Lee, "We'll meet you tonight at the cave."

Lee looked down the road once again. He watched as the trucks continued to stir up big clouds of dust. After you passed the footbridge, there was nothing on that road leading to the cove, and it was downhill all the way. Lee watched as the trucks finally reached the end of the road. They turned, drove onto the beach, and went out of sight.

The cove was one of Lee's favorite places. It was a beautiful, unspoiled stretch of beach on China's coast. It is halfway between Shanghai and Hong Kong. "No one ever goes down there at night, except fishermen," Lee thought. "And fishermen never come in a caravan of trucks. Those people are either lost, or they have business at the cove." He wondered what kind of business there would be in the dark of night on the beach.

Just then, Lee's mother interrupted his thoughts. "Lee. Get yourself in here. Everyone is ready to eat, except you."

Lee headed for the door, still wondering what was happening at the beach. He promised himself that he would know before the night was over. Little did he realize his whole life would be changed by what he would discover.

2

Smugglers at the Cove

It was already dark by the time the three boys finished their chores and met at the cave. They had the light of a full moon to guide them along the path. However, the darkness was not really a problem for the boys. They knew every twist and turn of the trail.

As they started down the path, Lee told Yung the story about the lizard that crawled out of the bush onto Kim's head. Kim made a face and said, "It gives me the creeps just to think about it! You know how I hate lizards. Why didn't it crawl onto Lee's head?"

"That's easy," said Yung. "The lizard didn't want to get lice!" Even Lee had to laugh.

They could not see the beach as they walked along the trail. But they could see the ocean beyond the beach. Lee stopped for a moment to enjoy the view. The full moon was reflecting on the ocean water as if it were glass. Lee thought to himself, "There couldn't be a more beautiful spot in all the world." Lee considered himself very lucky to live in China.

Lee spoke up. "Listen, guys. We're just going down to the beach to have a look. We are going to find out what is happening. But don't do anything silly. If we get into trouble, our parents will ground us forever."

Their mood was serious. Kim added his words of

encouragement. "Whatever happens, we've got to stick together."

Yung could not resist the opportunity to tease Kim. "Are you afraid we might run off and leave you, Kim?"

"We do need to stick together," Lee said. "But if something happens and we get separated, we'll meet back at the cave." Kim and Yung nodded.

At the bent tree, where the path turns and takes a steep drop down to the beach, the boys left the trail. They crawled quietly into the brush that lined the edge of the sandy hill overlooking the beach. They could hear the familiar roaring sound of the ocean waves. But louder than the sound of the waves, they could hear the noise that people make . . . lots of people.

When the three boys reached their lookout point, they looked to see what was happening on the beach below them.

"Wow!" said Lee. Kim and Yung moved their lips, but no sound came out. All three boys were stunned by what they saw. There were stacks of boxes near the shoreline. And people were streaming onto the beach to pick up the boxes and carry them into the grove of trees on the far side of the cove.

The boys watched as boxes were quickly loaded onto trucks and into cars. A number of vehicles were already leaving the area. There were bikes pulling trailers that were loaded with boxes. And people were riding bikes with boxes hanging on the back. They also saw people carrying the boxes, two at a time, suspended from the traditional over-the-shoulder bamboo rod.

"What's going on, Lee?" asked Yung.

"Well, it looks to me like we've found ourselves a ring of smugglers," replied Lee.

"Smugglers!" they echoed.

"Yeah. Very well-organized smugglers," Lee explained.

Kim asked, "How many people are down there?"

"There must be several hundred," Yung said.

"What could they be smuggling?" Kim asked.

"Look over there!" Lee pointed. "Isn't that our neighbor, Seng-Kee Ming?"

"No," said Yung. "It can't be! He's just three years older than we are. He wouldn't get involved with a ring of smugglers!"

"It is Seng-Kee!" Kim exclaimed. "I know it's Seng-Kee because he is standing there with his parents."

"You are right, Kim! That is Mr. and Mrs. Ming," said Lee.

Kim was stunned. "We have neighbors who are smugglers! I can't believe it. I've talked with them plenty of times. I've been in their house. I wonder if I've touched any of the stuff they smuggled? They seem so . . . normal. How could they do something like this?"

"That's a good question," said Lee.

"Look!" shouted Yung. "In the short time we've been here, those stacks of boxes have disappeared."

He was right. The stacks of boxes were no longer lining the shore. But the boys could still see hundreds of people working with boxes among the trees at the edge of the beach. Only a few people were still on the beach. One of them was Seng-Kee.

"Let's go down and talk to Seng-Kee," Lee suggested.

"He has to know what's going on. But what makes you think that he will tell us?" Kim asked.

"It won't hurt to ask," said Lee.

"You mean, you hope we won't get hurt if we ask!" Yung said.

The three boys jumped to their feet and headed back toward the bent tree. Lee led the way. Kim was trying to figure how many people they had seen on the beach.

"There were at least 450 people, if you figure 10 lines of . . ." Kim stopped midsentence when he saw Lee drop out of sight behind a bush. Then he saw several soldiers standing around the bent tree. Luckily, they did not see the boys.

Yung did not notice when Kim knelt quietly and crawled behind a bush. But he quickly realized he was completely alone. He wondered how Lee and Kim could have vanished. He decided to call them. As he opened his mouth, he saw the patrolmen standing just a few feet ahead. He gasped and sucked in so much air that he swallowed a mosquito. And when he dropped and rolled into the bushes, his "hiding bush" broke off at the ground and rolled along with him. Yung decided he would lie as still as he could.

The sound of Yung rolling around in the bushes attracted the attention of one of the patrolmen. The officer wandered down to where the boys were hiding. He walked right up to the bush where Kim was kneeling quietly, and began to look around.

Kim held his breath, convinced that he was about to be caught. He even started practicing what he would say to the patrolman. "Hello, Officer. I know this must look bad, but there is a good reason why I am kneeling behind this bush. This is actually a very funny story. And I'm certainly not a smuggler."

The officer came so close to Kim that his pant leg actually brushed against Kim's arm. As the officer leaned over, Kim was getting ready to stand up with his hands raised. "Look at this!" called the patrolman, as he held up a snake about a meter long. The snake

kept coiling and recoiling as he held it. Kim put his hand over his own mouth to keep from screaming.

As the soldier walked back to his patrol unit, he tossed the snake back into the bushes. The boys were breathing a sigh of relief . . . until the snake landed on Yung's stomach. This time, when the soldier heard rustling in the bushes, he thought it was the snake.

The boys listened as the patrol commander gave instructions to his men. "We are here to round up these smugglers as peacefully as possible. Use force only if necessary. After the violators have been arrested, we will destroy their merchandise. Now, move quickly!" The commander turned and led the patrol unit down the slope to the beach.

The boys crawled back to their observation point and watched the activity on the beach. The patrolmen were joined by other soldiers who helped them surround hundreds of the smugglers.

Lee watched silently as the patrolmen arrested the Ming family. The boys were horrified to see the soldiers beat some of the people until they passed out. The organized handling of the boxes had given way to complete confusion. The boxes were no longer being carted away, but the people were.

3

Pursued by Patrolmen

"Fire! Fire!" Kim was awakened by the smell of smoke. "Fire!" he yelled, shaking his sleepy friends. "Lee, Yung, wake up." It was still dark, so their attention was immediately drawn to the blaze on the beach. It took a moment for them to make sense of it all. Then they remembered the smugglers, the army patrol, and the arrests.

"We must have fallen asleep while they were arresting all those people," Lee said.

Yung stretched his arms over his head. "I didn't sleep very well," he admitted. "I dreamed I was hiding in the woods under a bush, and someone threw a snake on me! It was some nightmare!"

Lee looked at Kim and shrugged his shoulders. He whispered, "Maybe it's best if Yung doesn't remember that it really happened."

"That's quite a fire," Yung said. "To build the fire the soldiers had to carry those heavy boxes back to the beach. It's probably the hardest work they've done in a long time."

Just then, the wind grew stronger and blew out the fire. In great frustration, the soldiers began picking up the boxes and throwing them into the ocean. It was almost morning when the last box was thrown into the water, and the patrol left the scene.

Lee hit the ground running. "Come on! This is our chance!" Kim and Yung were right behind Lee as he moved quickly toward the bent tree. "This is our chance to find out what is in those boxes."

Lee turned onto the trail at the bent tree and followed it down to the beach. Kim and Yung followed Lee cautiously.

"Shouldn't we talk about this?" Kim asked.

"What is there to talk about?" Lee questioned. "This may be the only chance we ever have to find out what is in those boxes."

Yung stepped out in front of Lee. "You were the one who said we shouldn't do anything silly! What makes you think those boxes are worth the risk we're taking right now?"

Lee looked into Yung's eyes as he spoke. "Last night, several hundred people went to jail because of those boxes. We watched while they were arrested. They seemed to think it was worth it. Don't you think we should find out what they consider to be so important?"

"You are right," Yung agreed. He followed Lee to the water's edge. Then Yung waded out into the water and brought back one of the boxes. It was heavy. The three boys carried the box into the grove of trees. They stood in a circle around the box. No one spoke. Then Lee knelt down and opened the box. Kim and Yung joined Lee to get a closer look.

The boys gazed into the box with confused looks on their faces. Yung announced their discovery as if the others could not see. "Books! The box is full of books!" There was a long period of silence.

Then Yung jumped on top of the box of books. "When you go to sleep tonight, you can rest easy knowing that our land has been protected from the wickedness of books! The law has spared us from the

mischief of book smugglers and saved us from the evils of required reading and book reports."

Lee and Kim laughed and applauded Yung's speech. But in a moment the look on Yung's face changed. They realized it was a mistake to make all that noise. Two patrolmen were running toward them. Lee was holding one of the books in his hand. He quickly dropped it into his pocket.

The boys knew exactly what to do. They turned and ran toward the trail. The patrolmen were right on their heels. When the three boys got to the steep incline where the trail begins, they slowed down to turtle speed. Lee was the last to start up the trail. He was pushing Kim's rump with his shoulder. One of the patrolmen got close enough to grab the tail of Lee's shirt. But Yung and Kim made it to the top, and Yung reached out and grabbed Lee's hand and pulled him up. The sun was rising as the three boys started running up the trail with the two patrolmen in hot pursuit.

"Run, Kim! Run! Don't let them catch you!" Lee was running and yelling at the top of his voice.

The patrolmen were gaining on them. "Stop! Stop!"

The boys crossed the footbridge, where the path turned to the right. They made a sharp turn to the left and ran into the thicket of trees. They turned again, and ran into the high bushes that lined the edge of the stream.

"All we need now is another lizard," Kim whispered to Lee. The boys smiled nervously. But they were quickly reminded that they were in danger by the sound of the officers' boots hitting the planks of the old bridge. The boys crouched in the mud, under the cover of the bushes. When the patrolmen came to the end of the bridge, they followed the boys' path into the thicket. But again, they ran right past the bushes.

Lee, Kim, and Yung crawled back to the path. Lee was the first to spring to his feet and dart back across the bridge. But Yung and Kim were right behind him. When they reached the road, they ran up the hill and back to the cave, where they crawled under the blankets. It would be some time before any of the boys came out from under the covers.

Later that morning, before the boys went their separate directions, they promised not to tell anyone about what had happened. As the boys headed home, Kim was remembering a lizard; Yung was wondering about a snake; but Lee was thinking about a book.

4

What Is the Truth?

Word about the smugglers spread quickly. Everywhere Lee went that day, people were talking about what had happened during the night at the cove. All kinds of stories were told. Some were true. Some were not.

The Testimony of Bin

It started with his brother. Bin ran home announcing, "You've got to see it! You won't believe it unless you see it! There are thousands of books floating in the water. An army patrol caught some smugglers bringing them to shore last night. And the patrol dumped the books into the water."

"That's quite a story, Bin." Lee did not want to sound too interested, even though he was.

"Well, it's true. My friend, Park, told me all about it. The patrol surrounded the smugglers and arrested them. The smugglers were lucky they didn't get shot! But this is the best part. The books are floating on the water. Some of them are still in boxes in the shallow water. Right now there are fishermen loading the books onto their boats and bringing them to shore," Bin said. "People are taking the books so they can sell them back to the smugglers. Do you think our parents would let us keep some books to sell to the smugglers?"

Lee's forehead wrinkled, and he raised one eyebrow. "Let me see if I follow you, Bin. People were arrested and taken to jail for possessing some illegal books. You are suggesting that we collect and keep some of those illegal books. The same thing that happened to the smugglers could happen to us. And you think our parents are going to say this is a good idea! How can I say this so that you will understand? Not a chance, Bin! Not a chance!"

The Testimony of the Neighbor Lady

One of Mrs. Chang's friends came by to tell her what she had heard. "I have it from a very good source that the soldiers caught every one of the smugglers." She repeated herself very slowly to emphasize her point. "Ev-er-y one."

She continued. "The only ones that got away were the Russian sailors who brought the boxes to shore. The whole thing was a Russian plot to poison the minds of young Chinese patriots." She repeated herself again for emphasis. "A Rus-sian plot."

As Lee overheard the conversation, he knew that most of her facts were not true. But he was surprised to learn she knew one true piece of information.

She moved close to Mrs. Chang, as if she did not want others to hear. But she did not lower her voice at all. "They tell me the ring of smugglers included some of our own neighbors. You are going to be so surprised when you hear who they are! The whole family is involved in this awful business. Every one of them was arrested at the beach last night." As usual, she repeated herself for emphasis. "Ev-er-y one of them." Then came the painful truth that Lee already knew. "It's your good friends, the Mings."

The Testimony of Officer Woo

Officer Woo was one of Papa Chang's best friends. They had grown up together, and they often met to talk. Lee was sitting on the floor listening when Officer Woo talked to Papa about the smugglers.

"Were you on patrol last night when they caught those smugglers?" Papa Chang asked.

"No," said Officer Woo. "But I wish I could have been. This is the biggest case ever for the patrol in this region."

"Who was behind it?" asked Papa Chang.

"The fishermen who reported the operation said the men who made the delivery were Russians. But I doubt that," said the officer. "The fishermen may have thought they were Russians because they had beards. I can't believe that Russians would be making a delivery of Bibles."

"I didn't realize that it was a shipment of Bibles," said Papa Chang.

"Yes. There were thousands of Bibles. I can't imagine why anyone would want those silly books. Everyone knows the Bible is an outdated book of myths."

"How many smugglers did you catch?" Papa Chang asked.

"They rounded up several hundred people! If I hadn't seen them with my own eyes, I probably wouldn't believe it.

"We have been questioning them all day to find out who else was involved. You would think that out of that many people, someone would tell us what we want to know. But not these Christians." Officer Woo shook his head as he spoke. "They would rather stay in jail than tell us who was involved."

"What will you do?" asked Papa Chang.

"Oh, we will release most of them. We don't have room to keep them. But this isn't over. It won't really be over for a long time. We will keep making life difficult for those who were involved until someone breaks," the officer said. "Before it's all over, someone will come to their senses and tell us what we want to know. And we have ways to help them remember, if necessary."

The Testimony of the Bible

Lee had kept the book in his pocket all day long. Now he knew to call it a Bible. He wanted to read it, but he did not want anyone to know he had it. Lee could not forget the memory of hundreds of people who were willing to go to jail for the sake of a book. He thought to himself, "This must be some book!"

That night he took out the Bible and settled down to read. He turned back the cover and started reading at page 1. He read, "In the beginning, God created the heavens and the earth."

Lee thought to himself, "No wonder the soldiers were sent to destroy this book! Our government teaches us that God does not exist. They have told me that the world was not 'created,' but it simply happened. The Bible tells a story they do not want us to read." On that night, Lee read in secret for the first time about the seven days of creation, Adam and Eve, and the fall of humankind.

Before Lee drifted off to sleep, he thought about what he had read. There was a spiritual part of him that was in harmony with what the Bible says. Lee remembered from his reading that when God finished creating the world, He said, "It is very good." And as Lee thought about what he had read in the Bible, he echoed the words of God, "It is very good."

5

Hiking with Communists

"Wake up, sleepyhead!" Lee's mother called him from the door. "You've got a big day ahead of you."

Lee woke up thinking about what he had read the night before. "In the beginning, God created." Thoughts about God were new to Lee. It was like finding the missing piece to a puzzle. "Yes! The world was God's idea."

"Son, did you forget about the hike?"

In all the excitement of the last two days, Lee had forgotten about the big event. It was an activity for members of the Communist youth movement who were 12 years old. Lee, Kim, and Yung had been looking forward to this day for some time. Now he had to scramble to get there on time.

When Lee arrived at the footbridge, Su-Mee was giving instructions to the hikers. Su-Mee, the wife of Officer Woo, was the group leader and the guide for the hike. She was a tall, thin, nervous woman. She spoke in a high, shrill voice. Her huge lips were constantly puckered, as if she were ready to be kissed. And her eyelids fluttered as she talked. Su-Mee made her listeners squirm and feel very uncomfortable.

"We are taking today's hike in your honor," explained Su-Mee. "It is to recognize that you are growing up and are no longer little children. Now, use the

bathroom and wash your hands before we start down that long, long trail."

By the time Su-Mee had finished her greeting, even the most reluctant hikers were eager to get on the trail.

The hiking trail ran close to the stream. The hikers followed it closely. At lunchtime, Su-Mee called everyone together. "My fellow communists, I will give you two opportunities to show how much you are willing to sacrifice for our cause."

Lee noticed that Su-Mee had the habit of raising her eyebrows whenever she spoke. "Each of you has been in our community center for some kind of activity or meeting. We share the responsibility for taking care of the center. I challenge you to meet me tomorrow morning at the community center so we can do some work on the building and grounds."

Su-Mee bowed, and the hikers responded with polite applause.

"One more quick announcement. Four of our hikers left their lunches on the footbridge. This gives us an opportunity to prove what good communists we are by sharing our lunches with those who are more forgetful than we are."

The hikers spread out to find places where they could eat. Lee located a shaded spot and motioned for Kim and Yung to join him. As they settled on the ground, Yung explained how Kim had fallen into the creek. "Of course, he had some help."

Kim looked at Yung and laughed. "If I were you, I wouldn't walk too close to the water on the way back."

Before long they began to talk about the smugglers. Yung spoke, "I suppose you've heard some of the crazy things people are saying about what happened at the cove that night."

"I heard someone say the patrolmen killed some of the smugglers," Kim said. "We know that's not true."

"I heard it was a Russian plot," Lee told them.

"I suppose you found out that the books in those boxes were Bibles." Yung tried to sound matter-of-fact as he spoke.

"I heard that too," said Kim. "The soldiers are claiming that they destroyed all of the Bibles. Don't they know that most of the boxes were hauled away long before they showed up?"

"We know," Lee said. "We saw people haul boxes away by the truckload."

"Before this is over," said Yung, "we will know who planned this. And they'll pay for what they've done."

"What have they done that's so bad, Yung?" inquired Lee. "They brought Bibles so people could read them and make up their own minds about God. Is that so bad?"

"Of course it's bad," said Yung. "It's illegal. It's a sad thing when people think it's right to break the law."

"But what if it's the law that is bad?" asked Lee.

"I can't listen to this!" Yung protested.

"What is tragic is that people were denied the right to have Bibles in the first place," Lee said. "How can it be wrong for people to make up their own minds about the Bible? And how can it be right for the government to eliminate our choice when it comes to things like belief in God?"

"Because . . ." Yung noticed others were turning and looking at them. He lowered his voice and continued, "Because there is no God."

"If that is so obvious, then why should we be

afraid for people to think it through and decide for themselves?" Lee asked. "Tell me this, Yung. What will you think of your law if one day you find out there really is a God?"

"You say that like a Christian," Yung said.

"No. I'm not," said Lee. "But I have been reading one of those Bibles, and . . ."

"What?" Yung interrupted. "You kept a Bible, and you've been reading it?"

Lee looked down at the ground and answered quietly, "Yes."

"What has happened to you? Do you realize what you are saying?" Yung asked. "You are at a meeting of young Communists, and you're telling us you have been reading the Bible. Take a look at this picture of yourself, Lee. Is there anything in this picture that doesn't belong?"

After a long period of silence, Lee spoke to Yung. "It is true that I have been reading the Bible. I had never seen a Bible before that night. Reading it has caused me to ask some questions. I cannot close my eyes to the truth any longer. What I have read so far makes a lot of sense. I brought the Bible with me, and I was hoping we could talk about what it says."

"No, Lee! You know we can't do that," Yung insisted. "It is forbidden! You'll be in trouble if you continue to talk about it. And we would be in trouble if we listened to you."

"But Yung, the three of us have always talked about everything," Lee said.

"You're wrong, Lee," said Yung. "We've never talked about religion, God, or the Bible. We're not supposed to, and we're not going to."

Yung turned and walked away. Kim picked up his things and followed.

Lee spent the rest of the afternoon alone. When the hikers returned to the footbridge, Lee waited for Kim and Yung. He thought they would walk home together, like they always did. But Kim and Yung crossed the bridge and kept walking as if Lee was not there. Even though Lee called them, they never looked back.

In a few moments, everyone was gone. Lee was left standing alone on the footbridge. He waited several minutes, hoping someone would remember to come back and get him. But no one came. Lee walked home alone. He spent the rest of the afternoon alone. And he wondered if the hurt he felt would ever go away.

6

Walking with God

Lee did not eat much at mealtime. "Are you sick?" his mother asked. She felt his forehead to see if he had a fever.

Lee just shook his head. He did not feel like talking, so Bin answered the question for him, "I think Lee is in love. It's probably Connie. She's only about a half-meter taller than Lee!"

Lee gave Bin a look that told him he had better not say any more.

Mrs. Chang spoke to her husband as if no one else could hear her. "When Lee doesn't want to eat after a long hike, something is wrong. I think he might be coming down with something. If he doesn't have his appetite back in the morning, I'll stir up some herbs for him to take." Lee cringed at the thought of drinking one of his mother's herbal concoctions.

Late that night, when everyone else was asleep, Lee pulled out the Bible and began to read. He read the account of the brothers, Cain and Abel. He read about the descendants of Adam. But when he started reading about the great Flood, something happened. Lee began to see himself in the story.

When Lee read that God looked at His creation and "his heart was filled with pain" (Genesis 6:6), Lee understood. His heart was full of pain too. And the reason for his pain and God's pain was the same. They had been rejected by those they cared about.

Rejection is a difficult thing. It means to be refused, cut off, turned away. When Lee thought about the rejection of God by the Chinese nation, Lee knew that God felt pain because of them. Lee knew that God grieved because of them.

Lee read in the Bible of a time when people ignored God and lived in sin. Even though the people rejected God, there was a man who lived for and pleased God. His name was Noah. Lee read the story of Noah. He could not get away from these words: "Noah was a righteous man, blameless among the people of his time, and he walked with God" (Genesis 6:9).

Lee wondered, "How could a man remain righteous and blameless even though he was surrounded with people who rejected God and lived in sin?"

Lee asked himself, "When God looked at Noah, how was he different from the rest of the people?"

Lee decided the answer to both questions was the same. "Noah loved and obeyed God."

It occurred to Lee that his situation was the same as Noah's. The people who had been his friends did not want to be with someone who loved and obeyed God. They wanted to keep their distance from God.

Lee was thinking that Noah must have been a very lonely man. Then it hit him! How could he have missed it! Lee realized that Noah was not alone! He was not alone because he had a relationship with God.

Lee began to understand that God speaks to people through the Bible. And Lee was thankful for those unknown people who had risked their own safety to bring the Bible to him.

That night, 12-year-old Lee Chang prayed for the very first time in his life. He had never heard anyone pray. But it seemed to be the right thing to do. He prayed with his eyes wide open, *"I want to love and obey God too."*

7

Where's Your Bible, Preacher?

When Lee awakened the next morning, he knew his life was different. He needed to talk to someone about the changes that were taking place in him. He had tried to talk with Kim and Yung, but now he realized that was a mistake. They did not understand.

Lee made a decision. It was one of those little choices that would have big results for the rest of his life. His decision? He would leave things in God's hands. He had tried to do things his way without success. Now he would let God work things out His way.

As Lee walked to the community center for the workday, he thought about all that had happened since that night at the cove. He felt good when he thought about the things he had learned from the Bible. But he hurt inside when he thought about the way his two best friends were treating him.

As Lee walked toward the entrance to the community center, Kim burst through the door yelling, "Run for your lives! It's the grisly monster from the lagoon!"

Yung was running behind him, waving a mop and making weird noises. Lee could not help but laugh at the comical sight. Yung circled around Lee, and then

stopped directly in front of him, standing at attention with the mop on his shoulder like a rifle. Kim stood beside Yung.

"Well, look who's here!" said Yung.

For a moment, Lee forgot how Yung and Kim had treated him. He felt like he was with friends again.

Then Yung continued, "Look who's here. It's the preacher! Where's your Bible, preacher?"

Lee felt a knot in his stomach as he heard Kim repeating Yung's question. "Where's your Bible, preacher?"

Lee wished he could just disappear. But he said nothing, and pushed his way past Yung and Kim.

Once inside the center, Lee got in line with those who were waiting to be told how they could help. He could hear Su-Mee's shrill voice as she worked her way down the line of young people. She would flash a big smile as she spoke to each person. Then she would assign a job for each one to do.

She pointed to the tallest boy in the line and said, "Why don't you help the window washers? You may not even need a ladder."

To the girl standing next to him she said, "I love the outfit you are wearing. It shows you have a good sense of color. Take this paintbrush and report to the paint crew."

When she came to the Kwang triplets, she said, "You three are perfect for cleaning the high windows. Two of you can hold the ladder, and the other one can climb up and clean the windows."

She told several people, "You have such nice tans. You must like to be outside. You can help with the yardwork."

It took awhile, but Su-Mee finally came to Lee at the end of the line. He noticed that she called him by name. "Lee, you have always been responsible. I have a special assignment for you. Wait here until I come back." She went across the room.

As Lee waited for Su-Mee, he watched the young people working. Paint, polish, and soap and water were making the community center look great!

Then, as Lee looked around the room, he saw something he had never noticed before. He had been in the community center hundreds of times, but he had never seen the carved cross in the woodwork above the front door. He also noticed that small crosses were carved at the corners of the woodwork around each window.

"Crosses. They've always been there, in plain view, and I never even noticed them."

Just then, he heard Su-Mee's voice. "Lee, you probably know Seng-Kee Ming." Lee turned to see a smiling face.

"He certainly does know me. We are neighbors. Our families have been close for years, and our moms are best friends. Hi, Lee."

Lee had not seen Seng-Kee since the night on the beach when he was arrested with the other smugglers. Lee was so surprised to see him now that he found himself standing with his mouth hanging wide open. "Hi, Seng-Kee."

Su-Mee looked at Lee as she spoke. "Lee, I'm sending you and Seng-Kee to get some of the supplies we need today. Seng-Kee has a list." Seng-Kee nodded and the two boys were on their way.

8

"Everyone" Includes You!

"Well, Seng-Kee, how did you get roped into helping with this workday at the community center?"

"Actually, no one 'roped' me. I asked if I could help today," Seng-Kee answered.

"Why would you do that?" Lee asked.

"My family has been involved at the community center from the beginning. In fact, my grandfather helped others build the center. When I was young, my father was the caretaker. He loved that place so much. Last year, when dad decided he couldn't take care of the center anymore, I became the new volunteer caretaker."

"Maybe you can tell me about the crosses that are carved in the woodwork around the doors and windows. How did that happen?" Lee asked.

"Well, before it became a community center, it was a Christian church. After the Communist revolution, churches were closed. The government officials decided that religion was bad for the country. They said God does not exist. And they turned our church building into a community center."

"So your family takes care of the center because they still think of it as a church," Lee said.

"I suppose that's true. We keep hoping that someday the government will restore our religious freedom. And when they do, the church building will be ready," Seng-Kee explained.

Lee was quiet for a moment. He gathered the courage to ask some of his other questions. He took a deep breath, "What was it like to be arrested?"

"Oh. You heard about that," Seng-Kee replied.

"Well, I didn't really hear about it. I was there. I saw it happen," Lee confessed.

"Wait a minute. You were there when the patrolmen came and arrested us?" Seng-Kee asked.

"I was watching from the edge of the beach," Lee said. "I saw you moving the boxes off the beach into the grove of trees. I was there when the patrolmen surrounded your group and made the arrests. After they took all of you away, I saw the soldiers trying to burn the Bibles that were left. When that didn't work, I saw them dump the Bibles into the water."

There was silence as Seng-Kee tried to grasp all that Lee was saying. Seng-Kee shook his head.

Lee added quietly, "I kept one of the Bibles."

"What?" Seng-Kee asked.

Lee repeated, "I kept one of the Bibles. And I've been reading it."

There was a low stone wall at the edge of the road. Seng-Kee suggested they sit down to talk. "Lee, earlier today when we were with Su-Mee, I had a feeling that God brought us together for a reason. And I also had a strong feeling that you had something to tell me. So tell me about what you have read in the Bible," Seng-Kee suggested.

Lee started at the beginning. "I read that God created everything, and that Adam and Eve sinned. People forgot about God and became more sinful. So God sent a flood. But God spared Noah and his family. He spared Noah because he loved and obeyed

God. I've been waiting for God to send someone who could explain this to me, because I want to walk with God too."

Seng-Kee smiled at Lee. "Now I understand why God brought us together today. Lee, I have the best news you have ever heard. You can love and obey God. I want to show you in the Bible how God has made this possible."

Seng-Kee took his Bible out of his pocket and shared the Good News. "Lee, the Bible tells us in Romans 3:23 that all people have sinned and fallen short of what God meant for them to be." As Seng-Kee described the sinfulness that separates people from God, Lee knew that Seng-Kee was talking about him.

Then Seng-Kee turned to Romans 6:23. "This verse tells us that the natural outcome of our sin is death. But God, in His great love, has provided a way of salvation through the gift of His own Son, Christ Jesus."

Seng-Kee handed the Bible to Lee and said, "Read what the Bible says in John 3:16." Seng-Kee pointed to the verse.

Lee read the words out loud. "God so loved the world that he gave his one and only Son, that whoever believes in him shall not perish but have eternal life" (John 3:16).

Seng-Kee continued. "Lee, God provided a way for us to be saved while we were still sinners. We cannot do it on our own. We don't deserve it. We can't earn it. But God saves everyone who simply believes and calls on His name."

Seng-Kee turned the pages of the Bible and asked Lee to read the words of Romans 10:13. "Everyone who calls on the name of the Lord will be saved."

Seng-Kee explained, "Lee, 'everyone' includes you. All you have to do is ask Him to forgive you. Are you ready to ask?"

The expression on Lee's face told the whole story. Lee bowed his head and prayed, "Lord, I am calling on Your name, and asking You to save me, just like You said You would. Amen."

"Now," said Seng-Kee, "let me share one more passage of Scripture with you. These verses explain how you walk with God. The Bible says, 'God is light; in him there is no darkness at all . . . If we walk in the light, as he is in the light, we have fellowship with one another, and the blood of Jesus, his Son, purifies us from all sin'" (1 John 1:5b, 7).

Seng-Kee continued, "Lee, as you study the Bible, pray, and learn from other Christians, God will help you walk with Him."

"I understand," said Lee. "I will remember the joy I feel inside."

Seng-Kee suddenly remembered what they were supposed to be doing. "We've got more to talk about. But we better get those supplies to Su-Mee."

With that, they were on their way. And Lee was just beginning to find out what this new life in Christ would hold for a young boy in the People's Republic of China.

9

Under Arrest

After Seng-Kee and Lee returned to the community center with the supplies, Lee helped with several work projects. He washed windows, pulled weeds, and picked up trash. Lee had some difficult work assignments, but the entire day was an exciting, joyful adventure.

At the end of the day, as Lee was leaving the center, he heard Seng-Kee calling him, "Lee! Lee! I would like to invite you to come to our home tonight."

"I would like that," said Lee.

"My parents were some of the ones who prayed for that shipment of Bibles," Seng-Kee explained. "And they helped arrange for the Bibles to be distributed throughout China. Now they are being persecuted by the government for their involvement. I would like for you to tell my parents what reading the Bible has meant to you. It will help you to tell someone about your faith in Christ. And it will encourage my parents. Do you think you could do that?"

"Sure," Lee said. "I'd love to. What time do you want me to come?"

"The time doesn't matter," Seng-Kee told him. "Just come when you can."

When Lee arrived at home, his mother noticed that something was different about him. "You certainly are cheerful tonight. I expected you to come home tired and grumpy after working all day. But look at you! You are happy."

"It has been a great day," Lee remarked. He wanted to tell his mother about his commitment to Christ. But it was all so new to him that he did not know what to say.

Later that evening, Lee knocked on the door at the home of the Mings. Seng-Kee's mother, May-Jin, answered the door.

"Hi, Lee. You must be here to see Seng-Kee. Come in and I will call him," said Mrs. Ming.

Mr. Ming put down the book he was reading and greeted Lee. "Lee Chang. How nice to see you. You've grown taller since I saw you last," he said.

Just then, Seng-Kee entered the room with his mother. "Hi, Lee. Thanks for coming."

When they were all seated, Seng-Kee spoke. "Mom, Dad, Lee has something that he would like to tell you."

Mr. and Mrs. Ming gave Lee their full attention. Their faces were a reflection of joy.

"Well, I . . . I, uh . . . I don't really know how to say this. But I need to tell you that I saw all of you at the cove with the other smugglers. I was watching when the patrolmen came and arrested you," Lee said.

Mr. Ming spoke with concern in his voice. "We didn't know that you were there, Lee."

"It's OK, Dad. Lee has more to say."

Lee continued, "I wanted you to know that I took one of the Bibles, and I have been reading it. I asked God to send someone I could talk to about what I have read. And today, the Lord sent Seng-Kee to share the Good News with me. Now, Christ is my Savior."

Mr. Ming stood, raised one hand, and looked upward saying, "Praise the Lord!" His face was beaming.

"Lee, we started praying for your parents before you were born. And when you and Bin came along, we started praying for you too. This is an answer to our prayers."

At first, May-Jin sat quietly, her eyes brimming with tears. Then she placed both hands over her face and wept, saying, "Thank You, Lord, for those Bibles."

Then May-Jin spoke to Lee, "This makes me so happy. Your mother is my best friend. But I have never felt like I could talk to her about the most important part of my life, my relationship with God. I wanted to tell her about the Lord, but I never felt the time was right. The Lord is telling me now that this is the time."

"We would like to pray right now for you and your family, Lee," Mr. Ming said. The Mings stood in a circle around the chair where Lee was seated. Mr. Ming began to pray. "Lord, You know how Lee's salvation brings joy to our hearts. And we know that it brings even greater joy to You. We thank You. Now, Lord, show us how to reach out to Lee's parents and to Bin. Help us to . . ."

The prayer was interrupted by someone pounding on the front door. The pounding grew louder until Seng-Kee answered the door. When he opened the door, Officer Woo pushed his way inside with two patrolmen.

Officer Woo looked at Mr. Ming as he spoke, "Are you Chan Ming?"

Mr. Ming replied, "Yes, I am."

Then Officer Woo looked at Seng-Kee and asked, "Are you Seng-Kee Ming?"

Seng-Kee responded, "I am."

"We are here because you were involved in smuggling Bibles. You are both to come with me now for questioning," Officer Woo instructed.

"We have already answered your questions, Officer," said Mr. Ming.

"You will be questioned again," Woo replied.

"Then let us come by your office tomorrow at a decent hour," Mr. Ming suggested.

"You will come with us now either voluntarily or by force. It doesn't matter to me," said Officer Woo.

Mr. Ming kissed May-Jin. Seng-Kee said good-bye to Lee, and hugged his mother. Then they left with the patrolmen.

When the door closed, Lee and Mrs. Ming knelt to pray for the safety of Seng-Kee and his father. After praying, Lee hurried home. Lee's parents greeted him as he entered the house.

"What's happened? I can tell that something is wrong," said Mama Chang.

Lee explained, "I've been at the Ming's house. Seng-Kee and his father have been arrested."

"Oh, my! I've always been afraid something like this would happen to them," Mama Chang said. "They are Christians, you know."

"I know they are Christians, but I didn't realize that you knew," Lee said.

He looked at his father, who was shaking his head in agreement. "Yes. I know too, but only because your mother told me. The Mings have never said anything to us about religion. But we've known for years."

"It's probably one of the reasons we like May-Jin and Chan so much," explained Mama.

Papa Chang agreed, "They are the kindest people we have ever known."

"Where is May-Jin?" Mama Chang asked.

"She's at home alone," Lee said.

"I'm going to stay with her tonight," Mama said.

"And I will check with the authorities about Seng-Kee and Chan. Lee, you will need to take care of things here tonight," Papa said.

"OK," Lee assured them. "You don't have to worry about things here."

Papa smiled at Lee as he walked to the door. "I know."

"By the way, Papa, the arresting patrolman was Officer Woo," Lee said.

"That's good to know. That could help us a great deal," he said.

Lee stood at the door and watched his parents go out into the night to help their friends.

10

Release of the Prisoner

After Mama and Papa Chang left, Lee closed the door and turned around to find Bin rubbing his eyes.

"I can't sleep with all the noise," Bin said.

"Sorry, Bin. We didn't mean to wake you up," Lee said.

"While you were standing there holding the door open, I was freezing," Bin complained.

Lee admitted, "I wasn't thinking, Bin. I'm sorry."

"Hey, what's going on here?" Lee usually teased and pestered him.

"Bin. Something has happened to me," Lee said. "I want to tell you about it."

"What's the catch, Lee? You're playing a trick on me right now, aren't you?" Bin questioned this sudden change in his big brother. "You are only nice to me when you want something or when you are playing one of your tricks on me."

"Bin, this is no trick, and I don't want anything. Honest." Lee tried to convince his brother, but he realized he had mistreated Bin so many times Bin did not trust him. "Let me tell you what's happened to me, Bin. Will you sit down with me and let me explain?"

"I'll listen as long as there are no pranks," Bin said.

Lee started by showing Bin the Bible. He reminded Bin about the smugglers and explained that he had been there with Kim and Yung. He told Bin what he had learned by reading the Bible.

Lee told Bin how Kim and Yung had snubbed him, and how Seng-Kee had shared the good news about Jesus. Lee asked Bin to read John 3:16 and Romans 10:13. He explained that all he had to do was ask and he would be saved. The brothers prayed together for what would be the first of many times. Bin became a believer!

Later that morning, when Mama and Papa Chang came home, Lee and Bin told them, "We've got good news for you."

"We've got good news for you too!" their parents exclaimed.

That day, Mama and Papa Chang shared the best news that any parent could ever give to their children.

Mama Chang had gone to encourage May-Jin Ming. But May-Jin told her about Jesus, and Mama Chang became a believer.

Papa Chang had gone to help Chan and Seng-Kee Ming get out of jail. But Chan told Papa Chang, "You are the real prisoner, because you are a prisoner of sin." Chan explained how Christ could set Papa free, and He did.

That morning, the Chang family sat and listened as each member of the family told how they had come to believe in Jesus Christ.

After everyone shared their story, Papa Chang said, "I have an important announcement to make: Tonight, the house church the Mings attend is having a special celebration to thank God for the release of Chan and Seng-Kee from prison. We have been invited. Since this is a big step to take, I want each person in the family to vote either 'yes' or 'no.' The choice to attend is yours entirely."

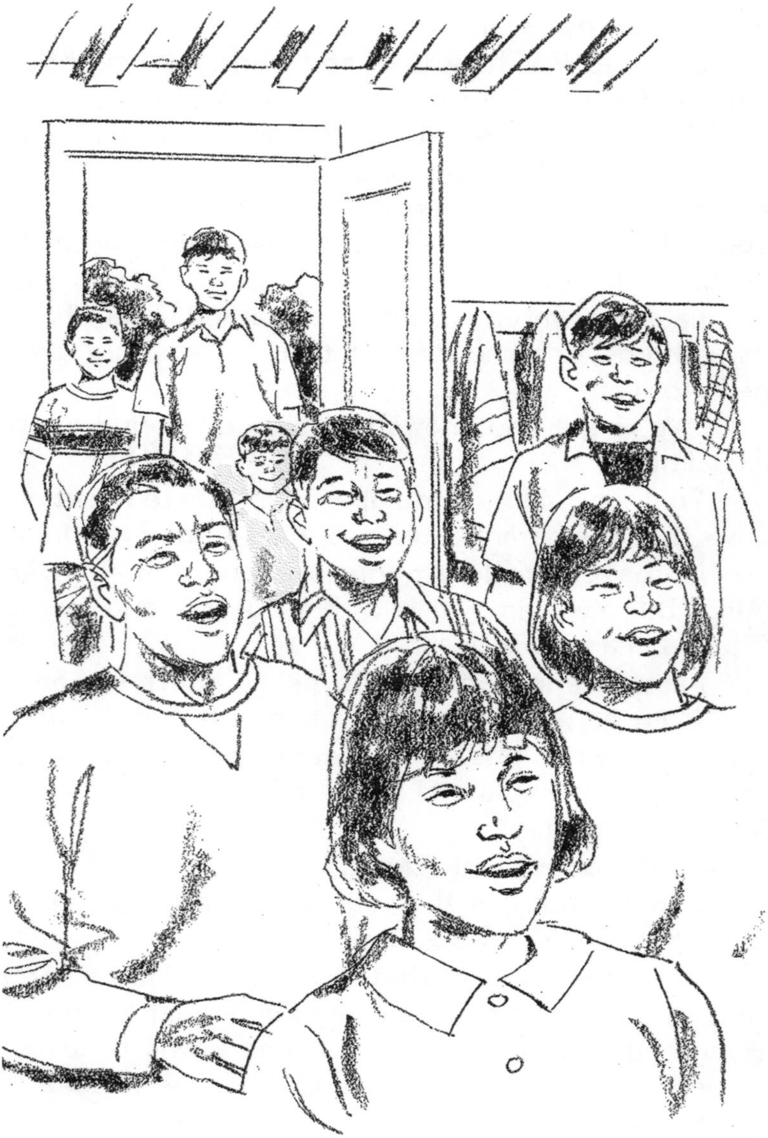

Papa asked, "How do you vote?" And the response was, "Yes." "Yes." "Yes." "Yes."

Since attendance at a house church is considered illegal, services are often held after dark. To avoid being noticed, people arrive at different times. And they come alone or in groups of two or three at most.

This house church met in a farmhouse that was a 25-minute walk from the Chang's home. The country setting helped to insure their privacy, because there would be little or no traffic in the area. That night, Mama Chang accompanied May-Jin. Papa Chang and Chan took a different route and arrived several minutes later. Seng-Kee walked with Lee and Bin taking a third route, and arrived even later.

Seng-Kee led the boys into a large room packed with people. The pastor stood and read words from Psalm 106. Lee would never forget those words of praise.

Praise the LORD.
Give thanks to the LORD, for he is good;
His love endures forever.

Then, the people quietly sang a song about being at home in the family of God. And Lee's heart said, "Yes! I am at home in God's family."

Epilogue
One Million Bibles

This story about Lee Chang and his family and friends is fiction. However, the account of smuggling Bibles into mainland China is true. Chinese believers had requested the Bibles. The need for Bibles was so great that the house-church leaders said they were willing not only to suffer but to die if necessary, so the people could have Bibles.

On the night of June 18, 1981, Open Doors delivered 1 million Bibles to a beach in a large cove. There were 232 tons of Bibles in 11,136 boxes! Twenty thousand believers helped to distribute the Bibles to house churches throughout the country, some as far as 3,000 miles away.

It is true that Chinese authorities destroyed about 10,000 Bibles, about 1 percent of the total shipment. But they were later replaced by the Open Doors group.

Today, a great revival is taking place in mainland China. Some estimates suggest that as many as 15,000 believers are being added to Christ's Church every day!

You may wonder how you can help. There is much that you can do.

- Pray that Chinese believers will have the Bibles they need.
- Pray for your Christian brothers and sisters in China.
- Pray for the pastors of house churches.

- Pray especially for Chinese believers who are persecuted for their faith in Christ.
- Pray that believers will be bold and continue to share their faith so the revival will continue.
- Pray that the leaders of China will hear the message of the gospel and turn to Christ.